W9-BRA-296

Getting Started in Science

Experiments with
Balloons .

Robert Gardner

and

David Webster

ENSLOW PUBLISHERS, INC.

44 Fadem Road
Box 699
Springfield, N.J. 07081
U.S.A.

P.O. Box 38
Aldershot
Hants GU12 6BP
U.K.

Library of Congress Cataloging-in-Publication Data

Gardner, Robert, 1929-
   Experiments with balloons / by Robert Gardner and David Webster.
      p. cm. — (Getting started in science)
    ISBN 0-89490-669-0
    1. Science—Miscellanea—Juvenile literature. 2. Science—
Experiments—Juvenile literature. 3. Balloons—Experiments—
Juvenile literature. [1. Balloons—Experiments. 2. Science—
Experiments. 3. Experiments.] I. Webster, David, 1930-
II. Title.   III. Series.
Q163.G2915 1995
507.8—dc20

          95-7035
          CIP
          AC

Printed in the United States of America

10 9 8 7 6 5 4 3 2

Illustration Credits: Kimberly Austin Daly

Cover Illustration: Enslow Publishers, Inc.

Contents

Introduction

When you hear the word *balloon*, you probably think of a party you have attended, perhaps one of your own birthday parties. In fact, balloons are often used to help people find a party to which they have been invited. Balloons are associated with fun, joy, and good times.

What you may not realize is that balloons can also serve as pathways to science. In this book, balloons are used for experiments—experiments you can do as you explore different gases, air pressure, electricity, buoyancy, floating, density, and other science-related ideas and activities.

Experiments with Balloons will allow you to carry out experiments using simple everyday objects and materials more often associated with play than with science. These experiments will lead you to a number of scientific discoveries, principles, and measuring techniques. They will help you to learn how science works, because you will be investigating the world as scientists do.

Some experiments will be preceded by an explanation of a scientific principle. In some cases, the explanation will involve doing additional experiments in order to help you better understand the principle. Once you understand the basic idea, you should have enough information to allow you to answer questions and interpret results in the experiments that follow. Some of these experiments might start you on a path leading to a science fair project.

A few puzzlers and surprises related to the experiments are scattered throughout the book. The answers to some of these puzzlers and surprises can be found by doing more experiments. The answers to others are located at the back of the book. But don't turn to the answers right away. See if you can come up with your own solutions to the problems or questions, first. Then compare your answers with the ones given.

The experiments and activities included in this book were chosen because they can be investigated by using balloons. Most of them are safe and can be done without expensive equipment. If an experiment requires the use of a knife, a flame, or anything that has a potential for danger, you will be asked to work with an adult. Please do so! The purpose of such a request is to protect you from getting hurt.

In France, on November 21, 1783, François d'Arlandes and Jean-François Pilatre de Rosier became the first humans to float above the earth in a lighter-than-air ship. They were lifted skyward in a basket attached to a hot-air balloon built by Joseph and Jacques Montgolfier. Ten days later, the French scientists Jacques Charles and Nicolas Robert made a similar flight in a balloon filled with hydrogen—the lightest (least dense) of all gases.

Balloons that Sink or Float

The experiments in this chapter are based on a science principle known as density. The following section will help you to understand density. Once you do, you should be able to explain the results of the experiments found in this chapter.

Science Principle: Density

Figure 1a shows equal amounts (volumes) of wood, water, and iron in identical containers. In Figure 1b, the weights of these objects are compared by placing them, two at a time, on opposite sides of a balance. Which object is heavier than water? Which object is lighter than water?

Now look at Figure 1c. Which object sinks in water? Which object floats?

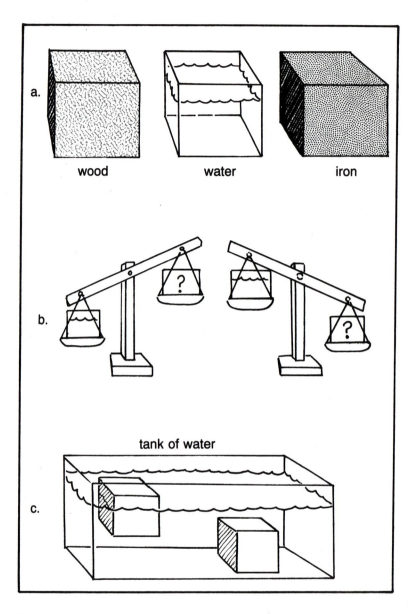

a. wood   water   iron

1a) Equal volumes of wood, water, and iron are placed in identical containers.

b) Which block (wood or iron) is heavier than water? Which block is lighter than water?

c) Which block sinks in water? Which block floats in water?

A material that weighs less than an equal volume of water (such as the wood) is said to be less dense than water. You might say that wood is less compact or less "pushed together" than water.

An object that weighs more than an equal volume of water, such as iron, is more dense than water. You might say that iron is more compact than water; it has more "stuff" packed within the same space. Wood is less dense than water. How do you know that it is also less dense than iron?

You have seen what happens when different objects are placed in water. Objects denser than water, such as iron, sink. Objects less dense than water, such as wood, float. You will find this principle useful in explaining what you observe in the next experiments.

1.1   RUB A-DUB-DUB, BALLOONS IN A TUB

A sink, pail, or bathtub is a good place to do some experiments with liquid-filled balloons. These experiments will help you to find out which things sink or float in water and other fluids. You will also see how temperature can determine whether an object sinks or floats.

To do this experiment you will need:
- 9- or 12-inch balloons
- hot and cold water
- sink, pan, pail, or tub
- plastic drinking straw
- salt
- twisties
- rubbing alcohol
- round and oblong balloons

1.1a COLD-WATER BALLOONS IN A HOT-WATER TUB

Will a balloon filled with cold water sink or float in hot water? To find out, fill a tub, sink, pan, or pail with hot water. **(Don't use water that is so hot it could burn you.)** Then attach a 9- or 12-inch balloon to a faucet, as shown in Figure 2a. Fill it with cold water until it is about the size of an orange. Use your fingers to seal off the neck of the balloon and remove it from the faucet. Carefully let out any air that may be trapped above the water in the balloon. Then tie off the neck of the balloon with a twistie, as shown in Figure 2b. Does the cold-water balloon sink or float when you put it in the hot water? Is cold water more or less dense than hot water? How do you know?

1.1b HOT-WATER BALLOONS IN A COLD-WATER TUB

Based on what you found in the last experiment, do you think a balloon filled with hot water will sink or float in cold water? To find out, place a balloon filled with hot water in a sink, pail, pan, or tub of cold water. What happens? Was your prediction right?

1.1c COLD-WATER BALLOONS IN HOT SALTY WATER

Put a balloon filled with cold water into a sink, pail, pan, or tub that is filled with hot water. As you have discovered, the balloon sinks because cold water is more

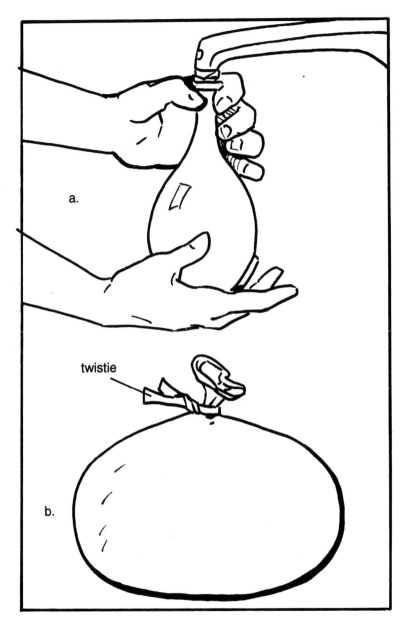

a.

twistie

b.

2a) A balloon is filled with cold water by connecting it to a faucet.

b) After any air is released, the neck of the water-filled balloon is sealed with a twistie.

11

dense than hot water. Now add a cup of salt to the hot water and stir. What happens to the salt? What happens to the cold-water balloon?

There are two ways to explain why the cold-water balloon floats after salt dissolves in the hot water. The first explanation is that the cold water in the balloon became warmer as it rested in the hot water. As it warmed, it became less dense and finally floated. The second explanation is that hot salt water is more dense than cold water.

A simple experiment will allow you to decide which explanation is better. Repeat the experiment, but this time dissolve a cup of salt in the hot water before you put the cold-water balloon in it. That way, the cold water will not have time to warm to a higher temperature. If the hot salt water is more dense than cold water, the cold-water balloon will float immediately.

Try it! Does the balloon sink or float? What does this tell you?

1.1d SALT-WATER BALLOONS IN COLD WATER

Fill a balloon with some of the salt water you prepared in the last experiment. Use a measuring cup to do this, as shown in Figure 3. Be sure to fill the balloon completely so that there is no air in it. With a twistie you can seal off the neck of the balloon. Do you think the balloon will sink or float when you put it in cold water? Test your prediction. Were you right?

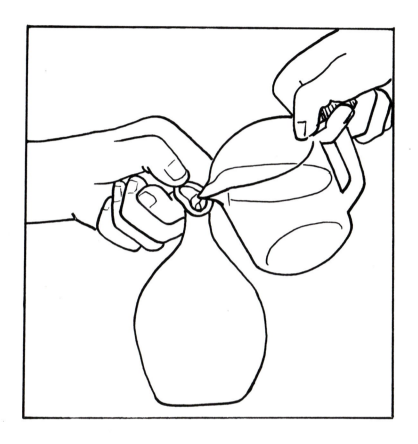

3) Use a measuring cup to fill a balloon with salt water.

1.1e   ALCOHOL BALLOONS IN WATER

Use a measuring cup to fill another balloon with rubbing alcohol. (Be sure to handle rubbing alcohol carefully, as it is both toxic and flammable. When you are finished with the experiment, **ask an adult** where to dispose of the liquid properly.) Seal the balloon with a twistie and put it in a pail of cold water. Does it sink or float? Is rubbing alcohol more or less dense than water? How do you know?

From this and earlier experiments, predict what will

happen if you put the alcohol balloon into salt water. Try it! Were you right?

1.1f   A BALLOON SUBMARINE

You can make a balloon submarine. Fill a balloon with cold water and seal off its neck with your fingers while you place it in a bathtub or a large sink filled with cold water. What happens when you release the neck of the balloon?

Which makes a faster-moving submarine, a round or an oblong balloon? Can you explain why? If not, you probably will be able to after you have learned about air resistance and area in Chapter 3.

To make a submarine with a longer-lasting "engine," use a twistie to seal the neck of an oblong balloon around

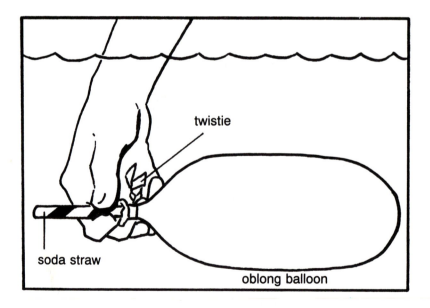

4) This balloon submarine has a plastic drinking straw as an exhaust nozzle.

a short length of plastic drinking straw, as shown in Figure 4. Why do you think this balloon can travel for a longer time than an open-necked balloon? What can you do to find out if a submarine with a drinking straw "exhaust" will travel farther on one "tank of fuel" than a submarine with an open-neck exhaust?

PUZZLER 1.1
During World War II, a number of oceangoing ships were made of concrete. Many ships then and today are made of steel. Yet both steel and concrete weigh more than an equal volume of water. How can ships float if they are made of materials that are more dense than water? Experiment 1.2 will help you to answer this question.

1.2   AN EXPERIMENT TO EXPLAIN A STRANGE FACT

To do this experiment you will need:
- modeling clay
- water
- sink, pan, pail, or tub

Take a piece of clay and place it in water. Does it sink or float? Does clay weigh more or less than an equal volume of water? See if you can figure out a way to make the clay float without adding anything to it.

If you succeed in making the clay float, you have an explanation for the strange fact about concrete and steel ships. What is it? How does your explanation compare with the one given for Puzzler 1.1 at the end of the book?

1.3 BUOYANT BALLOONS IN WATER

To do this experiment you will need:
- 9- or 12-inch balloons
- water
- sink, pan, pail, or tub
- Styrofoam
- paper clips or small washers
- rubbing alcohol
- twisties
- salt
- wood

As you have discovered, a liquid-filled balloon will float in a liquid that is denser than the liquid in the balloon. We say the balloon is *buoyed* (pushed up) by the denser liquid. The balloon sinks until the upward push of buoyancy equals the weight of the balloon and its contents. At that point, the balloon floats.

You can measure the buoyancy or "floating strength" of a balloon in water. To begin, fill a 9- or 12-inch balloon with rubbing alcohol as you did before. (Be sure to handle rubbing alcohol carefully, as it is both toxic and flammable. When you are finished with the experiment, **ask an adult** where to dispose of the liquid properly.) When you seal the neck of the balloon, turn the end of the twistie to make a hook, as shown in Figure 5. Place the balloon in a water-filled container. Add weights in the form of paper clips or small washers to pull downward on the balloon. How many weights can you add before the balloon sinks?

If you place the alcohol-filled balloon in salt water, do you think its floating strength will be more or less than it was in water? Try it! What is the floating strength of the alcohol-filled balloon in salt water? Was your prediction right?

Have you ever played with an inner tube, an air-filled raft, or a beach ball while you were in a pool, lake, or ocean? If you have, you may be able to predict how the floating strength of an air-filled balloon will compare to that of an alcohol-filled balloon. To test your prediction, fill a balloon with air until it is the same size as the alcohol-filled balloon. How many weights are required to make the air-filled balloon sink? Does air or alcohol have more floating strength? Was your prediction correct?

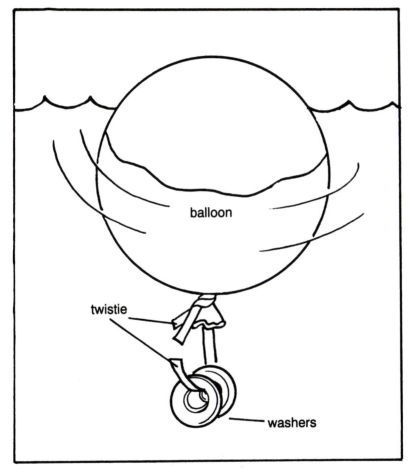

5) By making a hook on the twistie used to seal the balloon, you can add weights to the balloon and measure its floating strength in water.

Repeat the experiment, but this time put more air in the balloon. Does the amount of air in the balloon affect its floating strength?

Comparing Floating Strengths

If you want to compare the floating strength of wood and Styrofoam with alcohol, how big should you make the pieces of wood and Styrofoam? Once you have decided on a size, carry out the experiment. You can attach twisties to the wood or Styrofoam and add weights. How do the floating strengths of wood, Styrofoam, and alcohol compare? How do they compare with air?

To test the floating strength of the clay boat you built, you can place weights inside the boat. What is the floating strength of your boat? How can you increase the floating strength of your boat? What can you do to reduce your boat's floating strength?

1.4   BUOYANCY IN AIR

To do this experiment you will need:
- adults to help you
- thin (0.5-mil), large trash bag
- hot plate or electric stove
- potholders or oven gloves

You have seen that things which are less dense than water will float in water. Will something less dense than air float in air? You know that hot water is less dense than cold water. A balloon filled with hot water floats in cold water. Will a balloon filled with hot air float in cold air?

If you have ever seen a colorful hot-air balloon carrying passengers as it moves over meadows, woods, lakes, and even mountains, you know the answer. Hot-air balloons, like the one shown in Figure 6, use a torch similar to a blowtorch to heat the air in the balloon. Once the air in the giant balloon is hot, it is buoyed upward by the colder air that surrounds it. The principle is the same as a hot-water balloon floating in cold water. If a hot-air balloon begins to sink, the air within it is heated some more to keep the balloon aloft.

6) A hot-air balloon floats in the cooler air surrounding it.

Creating a Hot-Air Balloon

You can make a simple hot-air balloon. But you will need at least two adults to help you. **Have the adults** hold the open end of a thin (0.5 mil), large trash bag over a hot plate or one of the large heating elements on an electric stove. They should wear potholders or oven gloves and be careful not to let the bag touch the heater! You can hold up the closed end of the bag so that hot air can enter through the open end. Once the bag is filled with hot air, **have the adults** move the bag away from the heat and release it. What evidence do you have that hot air is less dense than cold air?

When a real hot-air balloon is filled, the balloon (or envelope), which is made of very light nylon, is spread out flat on the ground and attached to the basket that will carry people skyward. A powerful fan is used to blow air into the envelope causing it to partially inflate. The air inside the balloon is then heated with a propane torch. A nonflammable material surrounds the opening at the neck of the balloon to prevent the envelope from catching fire. As the air is warmed, it expands, filling the envelope and causing the balloon to rise off the ground. Once the balloon is floating, the passengers climb into the basket. The propane torch is then used to heat the air to a temperature of about 95°C (200°F) as the balloon rises into the air.

If the air inside the envelope is allowed to cool, the balloon will sink. To keep it aloft or to make it rise higher, the torch, which is connected to propane tanks in the basket, is used to heat the air and reduce its density.

1.5 PUTTING BALLOON SCIENCE TO USE

To do this experiment you will need:
- place to swim
- clear glass tumblers (2)
- eyedropper
- hot and cold water
- food coloring
- cooking oil

Understanding basic scientific principles, such as density and buoyancy, may help you explain things you can observe in your daily life.

1.5a   BALLOON SCIENCE IN A SWIMMING POOL

The next time you are in a swimming pool, exhale as much air as you can. This will make the balloons inside your chest (your lungs) as small as possible. With this small amount of air in your lungs, have someone estimate how much of your body is above water when you try to float in an erect (standing) position. How does the density of your body compare to the density of water?

Then inhale as much air as possible to make your lungs as large as you can. Why does filling your lungs with air make you more "floatable"?

Why do people find it easier to float in the ocean's salt water than in a fresh-water pool, pond, or lake?

1.5b COLORED DROPS, HOT AND COLD

Pour hot water into a glass tumbler that contains a few drops of food coloring. Place a clear glass tumbler filled with cold water near the colored hot water. Use an eyedropper to remove some of the colored hot water from the glass. Slowly lower the dropper into the glass of cold water until the tip of the eyedropper is near the middle of the glass. Gently squeeze the bulb of the eyedropper so that some of the colored hot water escapes. Why does the colored water rise to the top of the cold water?

Predict what will happen if you squeeze a drop of colored cold water into the middle of a glass of clear hot water. Try it! Were you right?

1.5c   OIL AND WATER

Pour about two tablespoons of cooking oil into a clear glass tumbler. Then nearly fill the glass with water. Let the mixture settle. Where do you find the cooking oil? Which is more dense, water or cooking oil? What other things that go on in the world around you can be explained by the experiments you have done with balloons and liquids?

On January 7, 1785, the French balloonist Jean Pierre Blanchard and his American copilot and sponsor, Dr. John Jeffries, became the first people to cross the English Channel in the air. They made the trip from Dover, England, to a forest near Calais, France, in a hydrogen balloon. Hydrogen leaked from the balloon, so by the time they landed they had thrown away all their ballast, their books, their instruments, and most of their clothing in order to stay above the threatening waves of the Channel.

Helium Balloons

You have probably seen helium-filled balloons at a party. You may have had them at one or more of your own birthday parties. In this chapter, you will use helium and other gases to fill balloons and carry out a number of experiments.

There are various places where you can obtain helium gas or helium-filled balloons. Your school may have a tank of helium that you can use for these experiments. Some science supply companies and many greeting card stores and supermarkets sell helium or helium-filled balloons. Helium is also available in small disposable cylinders or cylinders that you can rent for several days from many novelty stores. Other sources include welding supply or bottled gas companies. It will probably be fairly easy to find a source of helium in your area.

2.1   HELIUM AND AIR

To do this experiment you will need:
- helium-filled balloon *(Caution: do not breathe in helium—it can be dangerous.)*
- air-filled balloon

Obtain a balloon filled with helium. Use a bicycle tire pump to fill a second balloon with air until the balloon is the same size as the helium-filled balloon. Release both balloons. How do the densities of helium and air compare? How can you tell?

It is not possible to weigh a helium-filled balloon on a balance because it would float off the balance pan. In a well-equipped laboratory, a vacuum pump can be used to remove all the air from a rigid container. After weighing the empty container, it would then be filled with helium through a valve. A second weighing would show the container to be heavier after helium had been added. Such experiments show that helium weighs one-seventh as much as an equal volume of air.

Similar experiments reveal that hydrogen gas is even lighter (less dense) than helium. Hydrogen is only about one-fourteenth as dense as air or half as dense as helium.

2.2   A CLOSER LOOK AT HELIUM

To do this experiment you will need:
- adult to help you with Experiment 2.2a
- glass tumbler
- helium-filled balloons
- twisties
- string
- water
- plastic drinking straw
- sink, pan, pail, or tub
- birthday candles
- paper clips or small washers
- scissors

- helium *(caution: do not breathe in helium—it can be dangerous.)*
- helium-filled Hi-Float balloon
- cologne
- soap
- marking pen
- stopwatch or watch with a second hand
- trash bag or large clear plastic bag
- bus or car ride
- new pencil with eraser
- eyedropper
- clear pill bottle or vial
- 9- or 12- inch balloons
- modeling clay
- turntable or lazy Susan
- helium-filled silver Mylar balloon
- 250-milliliter (half-pint) wide-mouth jar

You know that helium is lighter than an equal volume of air. In fact, only one gas—hydrogen—is less dense than helium. You may also know that hydrogen will burn in air. Will helium burn?

To find out, you need to first explore a science principle. The principle, once understood, will help you to find out whether helium burns.

Science Principle: One Fluid Can Displace Another

A fluid is any substance that takes the shape of its container. A liquid is a fluid, so is a gas. Because most gases (including air) are invisible, you can see fluids displace one another most clearly by using water to displace air or air to displace water. Fill a sink, tub, or pail with water. Lower an inverted (upside down) glass into the water, as shown in Figure 7a. Notice that the air remains in the glass. Slowly tip the glass. You will see bubbles of air rise up through the water as water displaces air in the glass.

When the glass is filled with water, turn it upside down again in the water. Lift the glass so that only the

7a) When an inverted glass is placed in water, air remains inside the glass.

b) Water will remain in the glass even when most of the glass is above the water level in the sink.

c) Can water be displaced by lung air?

26

mouth of the glass remains under water, as shown in Figure 7b. Does the water remain in the glass even when most of it is above the water level in the sink?

Next, try to displace the water in the glass with a gas. Blow gently through a plastic straw, as shown in Figure 7c, to see if you can displace water with your lung air. Can you?

2.2a IS HELIUM FLAMMABLE?

To see whether helium will burn, fill a sink with water. Then fill a 250-milliliter (half-pint), wide-mouth jar with water. Invert the jar in the sink and use it to collect helium gas by displacing the water. You can do this by holding the neck of a helium-filled balloon below the mouth of the jar, as shown in Figure 8a. Carefully loosen your grip on the balloon's neck so that bubbles of helium can rise up through the jar and displace the water.

When the jar is filled with helium, **ask an adult** to light a birthday candle. When the candle is burning brightly, lift the jar from the water. Keep the jar inverted so that the helium cannot escape. (Remember, helium is less dense than air.) The adult can then raise the candle flame up into the jar of gas, as shown in Figure 8b. What happens to the candle? Does helium burn? Does helium, like oxygen, help to make other things, such as the candle, burn faster? Or does the helium put out the flame? Why do you think modern dirigibles and blimps are filled with helium rather than hydrogen?

Repeat the experiment, but fill the jar with air, not helium. What happens this time when the adult raises the candle flame into the jar?

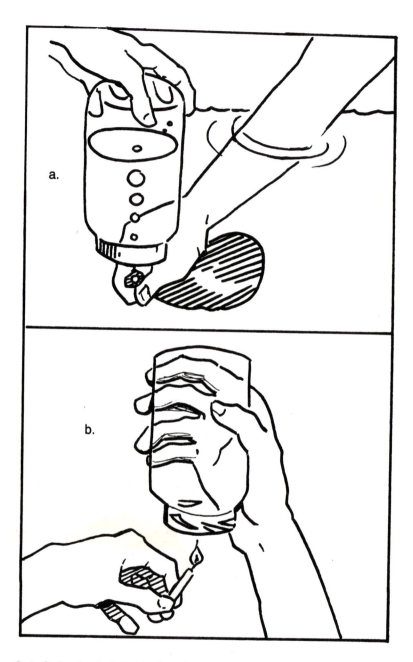

8a) Collect a jarful of helium by displacing water.

b) A burning birthday candle can be used to see if the gas is flammable.

2.2b HELIUM'S LIFTING STRENGTH

In Chapter 1, you measured the floating strength of liquid-filled balloons. You can do a similar experiment to measure the lifting strength of helium. Attach a twistie to the neck of a helium-filled balloon. Make a hook on one end of the twistie so you can attach paper clips or small washers to the balloon.

How many paper clips or washers can the helium-filled balloon lift? What else is the balloon lifting besides the paper clips? Do you think a larger helium-filled balloon will have more lifting strength? How can you find out?

Will two helium-filled balloons together have more lifting strength than one balloon alone? Design an experiment to find out.

Attach just enough paper clips to the balloon so that it sinks. Then remove one paper clip so that the balloon again floats. Now add a long piece of string to the balloon. The balloon will sink and some string will rest on the floor. The balloon will lift just enough string so that the weight of the balloon, paper clips, and string balance the upward push of the denser air. If you cut the string with scissors at the point where it first touches the floor, you will have a balloon that neither rises nor sinks. It behaves like a submarine in water.

On a dry (non-humid) day you may find that the balloon submarine will stick to the ceiling if pushed there. You may even be able to maneuver the balloon about the room by holding your hand near it. It will follow your hand. The balloon is attracted to your hand and the ceiling because of an electrical effect that you will examine in Chapter 5.

How can a balanced helium-filled balloon—one that neither rises nor sinks—be used to detect air currents in a room? Which way will such a balloon move near an open freezer or refrigerator door? Which way will it move near a warm heating vent or a radiator?

2.2c HELIUM'S FLOAT TIME

For how long will a helium-filled balloon float in air? Does its float time depend on its size? Does it depend on the thickness of the balloon? On the material of which the balloon is made?

To find out if size affects float time, fill two identical balloons with helium. Make one about twice as big as the other. Let both balloons rise to the ceiling and record the time.

Come back every hour or so to see if the balloons are still floating. For how long does each balloon float? Does the size of a balloon affect the length of time it will stay afloat in air?

Some balloons have thicker walls than others. Fill a thick balloon and a thinner balloon with equal amounts of helium. Let them float to the ceiling and record the time. How long does each balloon float? Does the thickness of a balloon affect the length of time it will stay afloat in air?

Influencing Float Time

Does a balloon that is twice as thick stay afloat twice as long? To find out, you will need three identical balloons. One of the balloons will serve as the thin balloon; the other two can be put together to make a balloon twice as thick as the thin balloon. To put the two balloons together, pull one balloon over the eraser end of a new, unsharpened pencil. Then carefully pull the second balloon over the first. You now have a balloon that is twice as thick as the single balloon. Fill both balloons with helium and measure their float time.

Buy a helium-filled silver Mylar balloon at a store. If possible, buy a helium-filled balloon that has been treated with Hi-Float (a gooey liquid used to coat the inside of balloons). Finally, buy an ordinary helium-filled balloon. Take them home and measure their float times. Which balloon floats for the longest time? Does the material of which a balloon is made or coated affect its float time? How far in advance of a party could you buy Hi-Float or silver Mylar balloons?

2.2d   SPEEDY HELIUM

When you release a helium-filled balloon, it rises to the ceiling. You have found that a big helium-filled balloon has more lifting strength than a smaller one. Does the speed at which a balloon moves from the floor to the ceiling also depend on the size of the balloon? Design and carry out an experiment to answer this question. What did you find?

2.2e   LEAKY BALLOONS

Since floating helium-filled balloons eventually fall, it seems likely that helium leaks slowly through the balloon. Even air-filled balloons shrink with time. To see if gases can pass through the walls of a balloon, use an eyedropper to add a drop of cologne to each of two ordinary 9- or 12-inch balloons. Fill one of the balloons with air. Fill the other with helium. Tie off the necks of both balloons and use a marking pen to identify the balloons.

Leaking Cologne

After several minutes, check to see whether you can smell cologne around either balloon. Can cologne pass through a balloon? Does the passage of cologne seem to depend on whether the balloon is filled with helium or air?

Continue to observe the balloons as often as possible over the course of a day or more. Does one balloon seem to shrink more rapidly than the other? If so, what does this tell you?

Keep the balloons for a week or more. For how long can you smell cologne coming from one or both of the balloons?

Watching Balloons Shrink

Repeat the experiment without the cologne. Does one balloon seem to shrink faster than the other? If so, what does this tell you?

If possible, repeat the experiment using identical

balloons, but this time use one balloon that has been coated with Hi-Float. Fill both balloons to the same size with helium. Compare the sizes of the balloons at the end of the day and the next day. Does Hi-Float affect the rate at which helium leaks from a balloon?

Will a balloon that is twice as thick (see Experiment 2.2c) reduce the rate at which helium leaks from a balloon?

Design and carry out an experiment to find out whether water can leak through a balloon. What did you find?

2.2f   HELIUM IN HELIUM

You know that a helium-filled balloon floats in air. In fact, a helium-filled balloon will rise to the top of an air-filled room and rest on the ceiling. But will a helium-filled balloon float in helium? To find out, you will need enough helium to fill a large trash bag or a large, clear plastic bag. Fill the bag with helium. Once filled, keep the open end of the bag down and the sealed end on top. Even with the bottom end of the bag open, it will rise to the ceiling. Remember, helium is less dense than air so it tends to rise into the bag rather than escape through the bottom.

Now fill a balloon with helium. Place it under the opening of the large helium-filled bag and release it, as shown in Figure 9. Does the balloon rise to the top of the bag or does it float near the bottom of the bag where the air meets the helium? Watch the bag and the balloon for a few minutes. What happens as helium slowly escapes from the bag? Does the balloon rise higher in the bag? Try to explain what you observe.

ceiling

large trash bag or
clear plastic bag
filled with helium

helium balloon

9) Will a helium balloon float to the top of a helium atmosphere?

2.2g   A HELIUM BALLOON ACCELEROMETER

An *accelerometer* is an instrument that detects changes in speed or direction. When a car starts from rest and increases its speed to, say, 80 kilometers (50 miles) per hour, it *accelerates*. If it then moves at a steady speed, it has no acceleration because its speed is not changing. When the car slows to a stop, its speed decreases; it *decelerates*.

You can build a simple accelerometer from a clear pill bottle or vial, as shown in Figure 10a. Fill the bottle with water. Leave a small space at the top so there will be an air bubble when you cap the vial and turn it on its side. Adding a tiny piece of soap to the vial will keep the bubble from sticking to the side of the vessel.

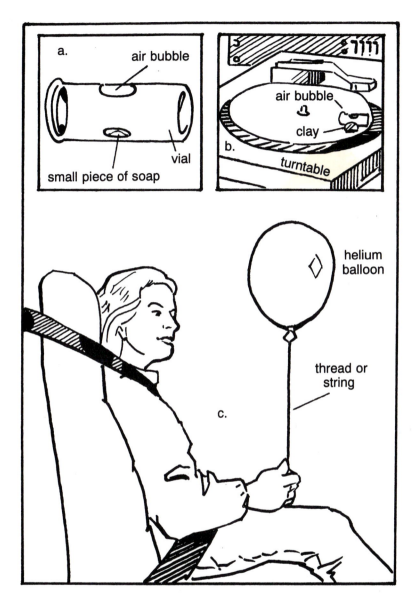

a. air bubble
vial
small piece of soap

b. air bubble
clay
turntable

c. helium balloon
thread or string

10a) An air-bubble accelerometer can detect changes in speed or direction.

 b) In what direction does an object accelerate when it moves in a circle?

 c) Can a helium-filled balloon be used as an accelerometer when traveling in a car or bus?

Detecting Acceleration and Deceleration

The bubble will always move in the direction of the acceleration or deceleration. To see this effect, hold the sealed vial in your hand so the bubble can move. Notice that when you move the vial forward, the bubble moves forward. As the vial comes to rest, the bubble moves in the opposite direction, indicating deceleration.

Now hold the accelerometer in front of you. Watch how the bubble moves when you turn around so that the accelerometer moves in a circle. As you can see, an object moving in a circle has an inward acceleration. You can see the same effect by using some clay to mount the accelerometer on a turntable or lazy Susan, as shown in Figure 10b. Which way does the bubble move when the table is turning? What is the direction of the acceleration on a merry-go-round?

Take a helium-filled balloon with you on a car or bus ride. Hold the balloon by a string in front of you, as shown in Figure 10c. Which way does the balloon move when the car or bus accelerates forward? Which way does it move when the vehicle slows down or brakes to a stop? When the vehicle goes around a curve? Does a helium-filled balloon make a good accelerometer?

In 1852, Henri Giffard, a French engineer, built and flew the first lighter-than-air ship to be powered by an engine. A basket suspended from Giffard's oblong, hydrogen-filled balloon held a small steam engine that turned a propeller. The ship, which could be steered with a rudder, was the forerunner of dirigibles powered by gasoline engines that were built in France and Germany.

Gases and Balloons

In Chapter 2, you found that helium is less dense than air, does not burn, does not help other materials burn and, unlike air, will put out a flame. You also found that helium will displace water and that it leaks through a balloon faster than air. In this chapter, you will use balloons to investigate the properties of some other gases.

3.1 CARBON DIOXIDE, AIR, AND HELIUM

To do this experiment you will need:
- adult to help you
- drill
- masking tape
- modeling clay
- 9- or 12-inch balloons
- plastic bags
- water
- yardstick
- string
- paper clips
- twisties
- bicycle tire pump
- seltzer tablets
- table or beam

- birthday candle
- 125-milliliter (4-ounce) clear flask or bottle
- matches
- 250-milliliter (half-pint) wide-mouth jar

Carbon Dioxide

Bubbles of carbon dioxide are released every time you open a bottle of soda. Animals exhale carbon dioxide when they breathe. The air we breathe into our lungs is 21 percent oxygen. Some of that inhaled oxygen is carried by blood to the cells of our bodies. It provides us with the energy we need to live and exercise. One of the waste products produced by breathing is carbon dioxide. It is carried by blood from our body cells to our lungs where it is exhaled into the air.

There is very little carbon dioxide in air. Most of it is used by green plants to make food. In the presence of sunlight, these plants combine carbon dioxide and water to make food.

Creating a Balance

To compare the weights of equal volumes of carbon dioxide and air, you will need a balance. You can make a simple but sensitive balance from a wooden yardstick.

Ask an adult to drill three holes through the yardstick, as shown in Figure 11a. The hole drilled at the 18-inch mark should be above the center of the balance beam. The two holes that are one inch in from each end of the balance—at the 1-inch and 35-inch marks—should be near the bottom of the beam, as shown. Insert a string through the middle hole. Use the string and masking tape to suspend the balance from a table or beam (see Figure 11b). Open two paper clips. Put the wider end of each opened paper clip through the holes near the ends of the balance. If the balance beam (yardstick) is not quite level, add a small piece of clay to the lighter (up) side. Move the clay closer to or farther from the center of the beam until the yardstick is level. To compare the weights of two objects, simply suspend them from the lower, narrower ends of the two paper clips.

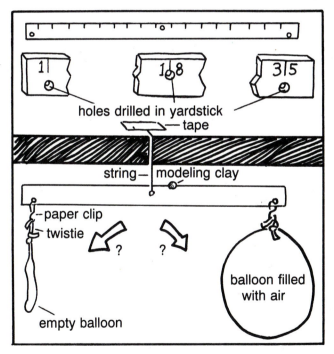

holes drilled in yardstick

tape

string — modeling clay

paper clip

twistie

?   ?

balloon filled with air

empty balloon

11a) Ask an adult to drill three holes through a yardstick, as shown.

  b) Add string and paper clips to make a yardstick balance that can be used to compare the weights of two balloons—one empty and one filled with air.

Weighing Air

You can use your balance to find out whether air has weight. Use identical twisties to hang two identical 9- or 12-inch balloons from opposite ends of the balance. If the two balloons are not balanced, add a piece of clay to the beam or use the piece you added before, and move it until the balloons are level.

Carefully remove one of the balloons from the beam and fill it with air from a bicycle tire pump until it is quite large. Then hang it back on the beam using the same twistie (see Figure 11b). Which is heavier, the empty balloon or the one filled with air? What evidence do you have to show that air has weight?

Repeat the experiment, using two identical empty plastic bags. You can fill one bag by dragging it through the air. If the temperature of the air inside and outside the bag is the same, the air will appear to have no weight. Like a submarine, it will neither sink nor float. Weighing air in air is the same as weighing water in water (see Experiment 1.1f). When air is forced into a balloon, the air is squeezed together by the stretched rubber. Because the air within a balloon has been compressed, it weighs more than an equal volume of air outside the balloon.

Collecting Carbon Dioxide

To compare the weights of equal volumes of air and carbon dioxide, you will need to obtain some carbon dioxide. You can make relatively pure carbon dioxide by dropping seltzer tablets into water. The bubbles that form are carbon dioxide gas.

To make and collect carbon dioxide, place about 25 milliliters (1 ounce) of water in a small, clear flask, (like the one shown in Figure 12) or in a small bottle. (An aspirin bottle that holds 250 tablets will work well.) Break two seltzer tablets in half and drop them into the water. Immediately pull the neck of a balloon over the top of the bottle or flask. You can see the bubbles of carbon dioxide being released from the water. Gas produced by the seltzer reacting with water will cause the balloon to swell.

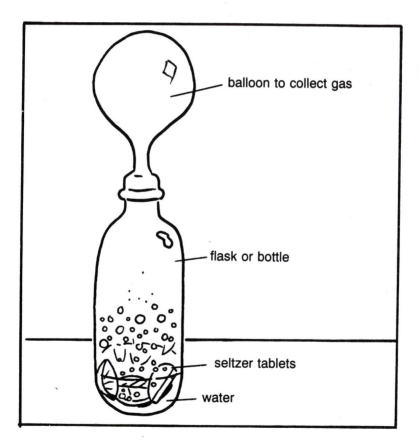

balloon to collect gas

flask or bottle

seltzer tablets

water

12) Carbon dioxide (CO_2) can be produced by dropping seltzer tablets into water.

Gently swirl the flask or bottle to release as many carbon dioxide bubbles as possible from the water. When the tablets have reacted completely with the water, carefully remove the balloon filled with gas from the flask or bottle. Be sure the mouth of the balloon is dry. Seal off the neck of the balloon with a twistie.

Weighing Air and Carbon Dioxide

Use a bicycle tire pump to fill a second identical balloon with air. Make it the same size as the one that is filled with carbon dioxide. Seal its neck with a twistie. Now hang both balloons from opposite ends of the balance. Is carbon dioxide more or less dense than air? How do you know?

Find two identical plastic bags. If you fill one with carbon dioxide and the other with air, which one do you think will be heavier? Design an experiment to test your prediction.

Remove the carbon dioxide-filled balloon from the balance. Collect the gas in a 250-milliliter (half-pint) wide-mouth jar as you did helium (page 28, Figure 8a). Because carbon dioxide is more dense than air, cover the mouth of the jar with your hand and turn it upright as you remove it from the water. *Ask an adult* to lower a lighted birthday·candle into the gas. Does carbon dioxide burn? Does it put out a flame, or does it make the flame burn faster?

In what way is carbon dioxide similar to helium? In what way is it different?

PUZZLER 3.1
Carbon dioxide is an *ingredient* in many fire extinguishers. Since both carbon dioxide and helium can put out fire, why don't we have helium fire extinguishers? Compare your explanation with the one on page 95.

3.2 AIR, "LUNG AIR," AND CARBON DIOXIDE

To do this experiment you will need:

- adult to help you
- water
- sink, pan, pail, or tub
- seltzer tablets
- bicycle tire pump
- yardstick balance
- 125-milliliter (4-ounce) clear flask or bottle
- 9- or 12-inch balloons
- plastic drinking straw
- birthday candle
- matches
- twisties
- plastic drinking straw
- 250-milliliter (half-pint) wide-mouth jar

You might think that the air you breathe out of your lungs is very similar to carbon dioxide. After all, the carbon dioxide released from all the cells of your body is carried by blood to your lungs.

You found earlier that a birthday candle flame is quickly extinguished in carbon dioxide. In air, the flame continues to burn as expected. What do you think will happen when a burning birthday candle is placed in lung air?

Collecting Lung Air

To find out, collect some lung air by blowing into a balloon. Then collect the lung air in a 250-milliliter (half-pint) wide-mouth jar (as you collected helium on page 28,

Figure 8a). You don't know whether lung air is more dense or less dense than air, so first assume it is more dense. Cover the mouth of the jar with your hand and turn it upright as you remove it from the water. **Ask an adult** to lower a lighted birthday candle into the gas. Does lung air burn? Does it put out a flame or make it burn faster?

Collect another jarful of lung air. This time assume it is less dense than air. Keep the mouth of the jar turned downward when you remove it from the water. **Ask an adult** to raise a burning birthday candle up into the jar. Does lung air burn? Does it put out a flame or make it burn faster?

Comparing Densities

To find out how the densities of air, lung air, and carbon dioxide compare, you will need three identical balloons. Fill one balloon with carbon dioxide, as you did in Experiment 3.1. Fill a second balloon with the same amount of air using a bicycle tire pump. Fill the third balloon with the same volume of lung air. To be sure no saliva enters the lung air-filled balloon, which would add to its weight, do the following: place a plastic drinking straw in the neck of the balloon (see Figure 13), and wrap a twistie around the balloon to secure it to the straw. Then blow upward through the straw to fill the balloon.

Compare the weights of the three balloons on the balance you used in Experiment 3.1. How do the densities of lung air and carbon dioxide compare? How do the densities of lung air and air compare?

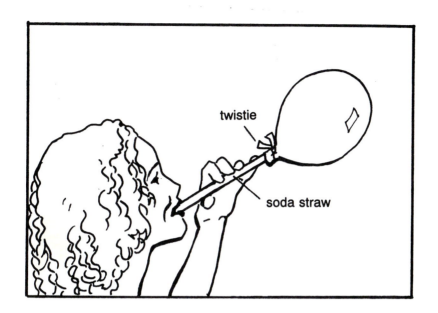

twistie

soda straw

13) To fill a balloon with lung air, blow upward through a straw to prevent saliva from entering the balloon.

3.3   MORE LEAKING BALLOONS

To do this experiment you will need:
- 9- or 12-inch balloons
- twisties
- bicycle tire pump
- new pencil with eraser
- water
- seltzer tablets
- plastic drinking straw
- 125-milliliter (4-ounce) clear flask or bottle

Fill one of three identical balloons with carbon dioxide. Use seltzer tablets and water to produce the carbon dioxide, as you did in Experiment 3.1. Use a bicycle tire pump to fill a second balloon with an equal volume of air. Fill a third balloon with the same volume of lung air. To avoid getting saliva in the balloon, use a plastic soda straw and twistie, as you did in Experiment 3.2.

Label the balloons in some way so you know which gas is in each balloon.

Leave all three balloons in the same place. Observe them from time to time for several days. Does one balloon seem to shrink faster than the others? Do you observe any other differences in the balloons?

Will doubling the thickness of a balloon reduce the leaking rate of carbon dioxide? To find out, make a double-layered balloon (see Experiment 2.2c) and fill it with carbon dioxide. Fill a single layered balloon with the same amount of the gas. Compare the rate at which the two balloons leak carbon dioxide. Does thickness affect the rate at which carbon dioxide leaks from a balloon?

3.4   FALLING BALLOONS

To do this experiment you will need:
- 9- or 12-inch balloons
- twisties
- bicycle tire pump
- 125-milliliter (4-ounce) clear flask or bottle
- water
- seltzer tablets
- plastic drinking straw
- marking pen

Again, fill three identical balloons with equal volumes of carbon dioxide, air, and lung air. Label the balloons with a marking pen so you can identify which gas is in each one. Based on what you learned in Experiment 3.1, which balloon is the heaviest? Which balloon do you think will fall fastest?

To test your prediction, drop the balloons two at a time from the same height. Do this several times to be sure the results are consistent. Does one balloon fall faster than the others?

Based on the experiments you have done, is lung air more like air or carbon dioxide? What makes you think so?

SURPRISE 3.1
The results of Experiment 3.4 may have surprised you because you may have learned that all things fall at the same rate. If you drop a baseball and a tennis ball from the same height at the same time, they will fall side by side. They will reach the floor at the same instant. If you have never tried this experiment, do it now. Do you agree that the two balls fall side by side?

Science Principle: Air Resistance and Area

As long as you drop reasonably small, heavy objects through short distances, they will fall side by side. In a vacuum, where there is no air, all objects fall at the same rate no matter what their size or weight. When an object falls in air, the gas pushes upward against it. This push is called *air resistance*. It keeps the object from falling as fast as it would in a vacuum.

To see how the *area* (the amount of surface) affects air resistance, try this: Take two sheets of paper. Crumple one sheet into a tight ball. Leave the other sheet flat. Drop both pieces of paper at the same time. Which one falls faster? How does the amount of area (surface) affect the air resistance of a falling object?

A heavy object weighs so much that it can overcome

much of the air resistance early in its fall. To see this for yourself, place the sheet of paper on a book. The book should be wider and longer than the paper, as shown Figure 14. Drop the book with the paper on top so air can't touch the bottom of the paper. Do book and paper fall together? What do you think will happen if you drop book and paper separately? Try it! Were you right?

14) How does a book that shields a sheet of paper from air resistance affect the paper's rate of fall?

3.5   FALLING BALLOONS AND TERMINAL SPEEDS

To do this experiment you will need:
- adult to help you
- twisties
- bicycle tire pump
- tape measure
- stopwatch or watch with a second hand
- round and oblong balloons
- water
- seltzer tablets
- plastic drinking straw
- new pencil with eraser
- 125-milliliter (4-ounce) clear flask or bottle

Air Resistance

Normally, when an object falls, air resistance prevents it from falling as fast as it would in a vacuum. As the speed of the falling object increases, the air resistance pushing upward on the object increases too. If it falls long enough, its speed will increase until the air resistance becomes equal to its weight. When weight and air resistance are equal, the object falls at a constant speed known as the *terminal velocity*.

After jumping from an airplane, a skydiver accelerates downward. To increase air resistance, he or she may assume a "spread eagle" position with arms and legs outstretched. Such a position offers as much body area as possible to the air and increases air resistance. After falling for 10 seconds or less, a skydiver reaches a terminal velocity of about 190 kilometers (120 miles) per hour, which is the same as 53 meters per second (173 feet per second).

Measuring Terminal Velocity

A balloon reaches a terminal velocity almost as soon as it begins to fall. To find a balloon's terminal velocity, **ask an adult** to hold a balloon near the ceiling. Use a tape measure to find the distance between the bottom of the balloon and the floor. Have the adult drop the balloon when you say, "Go!" At the same moment, start a stopwatch. When the balloon reaches the floor, stop the watch. Repeat the experiment several times to be sure the results are consistent.

If you don't have a stopwatch, count, "1, 2, 3, 4, 5," as fast as you can while the balloon is falling. You will find that it takes just about one second to count to 5 very fast. Try counting to 5 ten times. It should take just about ten seconds. If you count to 5 three times while the balloon falls to the floor, it took three seconds for the balloon to fall. If you counted to 5 three times and then got to 2 on the fourth count, it took the balloon 3.4 seconds to reach the floor.

To find the terminal velocity of the balloon, divide the distance the balloon fell by the time it took to fall that distance. For example, if the balloon fell 7 feet in 3.4 seconds, you can find the terminal velocity by using a pocket calculator to divide 7 feet by 3.4 seconds. You would find the velocity to be about 2.1 feet per second.

Influencing Terminal Velocity

Do some experiments to find out how each of the following affect a balloon's terminal velocity:
- the size of the balloon
- the kind of gas in the balloon (see Experiment 3.2)
- the weight of the balloon
- the shape of the balloon
- the thickness of the balloon's wall (see Experiment 2.2c)

During World War I, German Zeppelins subjected England to the first large-scale aerial bombings in history. To combat these high-flying, hydrogen-filled, lighter-than-air ships, the British developed airplanes that could fly as high as the Zeppelins. By firing tracer bullets into the Zeppelins, the British planes could often ignite the hydrogen in the Zeppelins.

Balloons, Gases, Temperature, and Pressure

Balloons are a good way to investigate how temperature and pressure affect a gas. Temperature is a measure of how warm or cold something is. It can be determined with a thermometer. The most common use of a thermometer is to measure the temperature of the air.

Pressure is the push (force) that something exerts on the area that it touches. When you stand on a floor, the pressure you exert on the floor is your weight spread over the area of your shoes. Pressure is usually measured in pounds per square inch or newtons per square meter. A barometer, manometer, or gauge (such as the kind found in an aneroid barometer) can be used to measure pressure.

4.1 GASES AND TEMPERATURE

To do this experiment you will need:
- pail
- 9-or 12-inch balloons
- 1-quart narrow-mouth glass bottle
- hot and cold water
- freezer
- new pencil with eraser

Raising the Temperature

In this experiment, you can see how a gas is affected by changes in temperature. Begin the experiment by filling a pail with hot water. Attach an empty 9- or 12-inch balloon to the neck of a narrow-mouth, 1-quart glass bottle, as shown in Figure 15. Place the bottle in

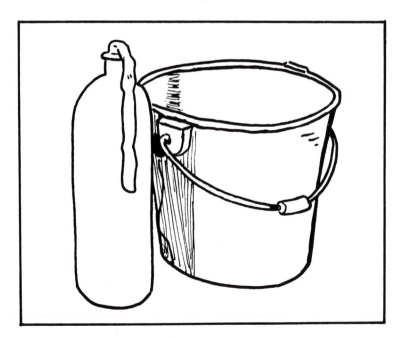

15) A balloon attached to a bottle can be used to find out what happens to a gas when its temperature changes.

the pail of hot water. What happens to the balloon? What happens to the volume of a gas when its temperature rises?

Remove the bottle from the hot water and let it cool for a few minutes. What happens to the balloon as the air in the bottle cools?

Now take the balloon off the bottle. Rinse the bottle several times with hot water. The heated bottle will warm the air that enters the bottle after the water is poured out. Put the empty balloon back on the bottle of warm air. What happens to the balloon as the air inside the bottle cools?

Lowering the Temperature

To lower the temperature of the gas in the bottle even more, place the bottle in a pail of cold water. What happens to the balloon now? If the balloon seems to want to turn inside-out and enter the bottle, use the eraser end of a pencil to guide the balloon so it doesn't get stuck.

Place the bottle and balloon in a freezer where the temperature of the air in the bottle will drop to well below 0°C (32°F). After about 10 minutes, look at the bottle and balloon. What has happened? What happened to the volume of the air in the bottle when its temperature dropped?

Remove the bottle from the freezer. What do you think will happen as the air in the bottle warms back to the temperature of the room?

Expansion and Contraction

You have seen air expand when heated and contract when cooled. The results would have been the same if the bottle had been filled with any gas—carbon dioxide, helium, oxygen, hydrogen, etc. All gases expand and contract in the same way with changes in temperature.

As you know, a balloon tends to squeeze a gas together. If you fill a balloon with gas and then release it, the gas is quickly squeezed from the balloon. The pressure created inside the balloon by its stretched rubber wall is greater than the pressure of the air outside the balloon. As a result, the gas is pushed out through the neck of the balloon.

In Experiment 4.1, the changes in the volume of a gas were affected by pressure, as well as by temperature. In the following two science principles, you will examine how each of these factors alone affects the volume of a gas.

Science Principle: The Volume of a Gas and its Temperature

In this experiment, you will see how the volume of a gas is related to temperature when the pressure stays the same. To begin, hold a clear plastic drinking straw sideways. Use an eyedropper to inject a drop of water into one end of the straw. Gently tilt the straw upward and let the water plug slide about 4 centimeters (1.5 inches) down the straw. Without moving the water plug, pinch and flatten about 2.5 centimeters (1 inch) of the straw at its lower end. Fold the end over, as shown in Figure

16, and wrap it firmly with masking tape. Use a marking pen to make a line on the straw at the lower end of the water plug. You now have a small volume of air trapped between the sealed lower end of the straw and the water plug.

Place the straw in an upright position in the freezing compartment of your refrigerator. After several minutes, remove the straw and look at the position of the water

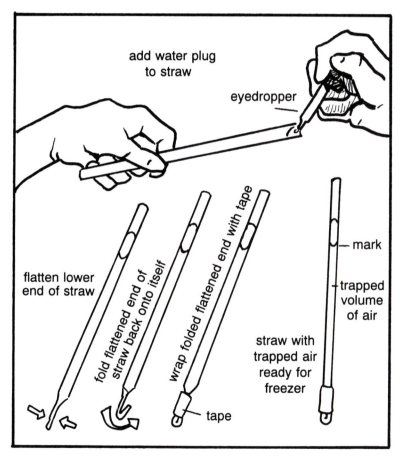

add water plug
to straw

eyedropper

flatten lower
end of straw

fold flattened end of
straw back onto itself

wrap folded flattened end with tape

mark

trapped
volume
of air

straw with
trapped air
ready for
freezer

tape

16) This simple instrument can be used to see what happens to the volume of a gas when its temperature changes without any change in pressure.

plug. Has the volume of the air in the straw changed? How do you know? What happens to the volume of a gas when its temperature decreases?

To see what happens when the temperature of the trapped air increases, place the tube upright in a glass of hot water. Observe how the water plug moves. What happens to the volume of a gas when its temperature rises?

Science: The Volume of a Gas and its Pressure

You can use a plastic syringe to see how the volume of a gas is related to pressure when the temperature doesn't change. Set the piston in the syringe at about the middle of the cylinder, as shown in Figure 17. Hold your finger firmly over the opening in the bottom of the syringe. Slowly push down on the piston with your other hand. You can feel the pressure of the air—the force it exerts on the bottom area of the piston—grow larger. As you can see, the air below the piston is squeezed into a smaller volume. The piston pushing the gas together is similar to the rubber walls of a stretched balloon squeezing a gas together. As the volume of a gas grows smaller by squeezing it together, what happens to the pressure exerted by the gas?

Robert Boyle, a seventeenth-century scientist, discovered that if you compress a gas until its volume is half as big, the pressure exerted by the gas will be twice as much.

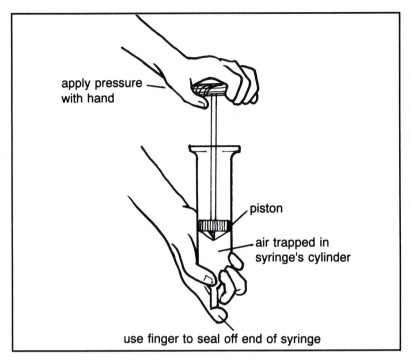

apply pressure
with hand

piston

air trapped in
syringe's cylinder

use finger to seal off end of syringe

17) An empty plastic syringe can be used to see how the volume of a gas changes with pressure when the temperature is constant.

4.2 BALLOONS, GASES, AND PRESSURE

To do this experiment you will need:
- water
- clear glass tumbler
- scissors
- cardboard

In Chapter 2, you learned that one fluid can displace another. In experiment 2.2, you found you could lift a water-filled glass until its mouth was just below the water level in a sink or pail. What you may not know is that the water in the glass was held up by the pressure of the air pushing on the surface of the liquid.

The Effect of Air Pressure

To see the effect of air pressure more directly, try this. Fill a glass to the brim with water. Find a piece of cardboard that is slightly larger than the mouth of the glass. Wet the cardboard with water. Then slide it over the mouth of the water-filled glass. Place your hand on the cardboard and invert the glass (turn it upside down) over a sink. You will find that you can remove your hand. Air pressure will hold the cardboard against the glass and support the water column in the glass. In fact, air pressure will support a column of water nearly 10.3 meters (34 feet) high at sea level. (The pressure of the air will lessen the higher you go into the atmosphere.)

Although 34-foot barometers have been built, they are not very practical. Consequently, mercury (not water) is used in barometers. Because mercury is 13.5 times as dense as water, the mercury in a barometer stands only 76 centimeters (30 inches) high at sea level.

Before you do another experiment to show that air exerts pressure, first look at two more science principles related to gas pressure.

Science Principle: Gas Pressure and Temperature

Figure 18 shows the pressure of a gas as its temperature changes. The thermometers, of course, measure the temperature of the gas; the gauges measure the gas pressure. What happens to the pressure as the temperature rises? What happens to the pressure as the temperature drops?

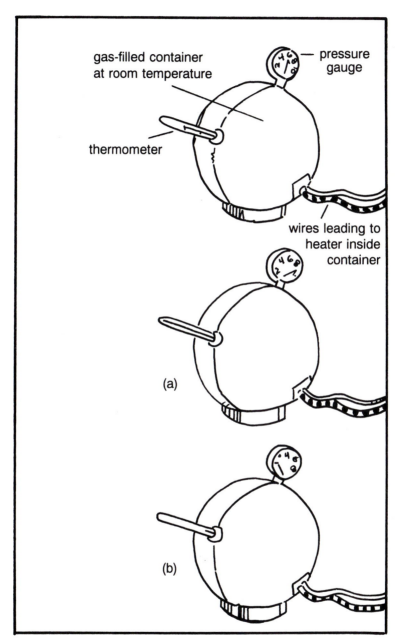

gas-filled container at room temperature

pressure gauge

thermometer

wires leading to heater inside container

(a)

(b)

18) A thermometer and pressure gauge show what happens to the pressure of a fixed volume of gas when the temperature (a) rises and (b) falls.

Science Principle: Air Will Fill an Empty Space

An empty space is one that contains nothing. If you open a door and walk into a room that has no rugs, furniture, or curtains, the room is not empty; it is filled with air. If the air were pumped out of the room, then it would be empty. However, pumping the air from the room would cause the walls to collapse. You will understand why after you do Experiment 4.3.

Figure 19a shows a large, sturdy, thick-walled bottle that is filled with air. The bottle is connected on one side to a plastic bag filled with air. A faucet-like valve in the tube connecting the bottle to the bag of air can be opened or closed. When it is open, air can flow between the bottle and the plastic bag. A similar valve is found between the bottle and a pump. When this valve is open, the pump can remove practically all the air from the bottle. After the bottle is emptied, the valve connecting the pump to the bottle can be closed. If the valve connecting the bottle to the plastic bag is then opened, air will flow from the bag to the bottle, as shown in Figure 19b.

In Figure 19c, the bottle is replaced with a thin-walled metal can. Normally, the pressure of the air inside and outside an empty can are the same and so the can maintains its shape. However, if the valve between the can and the plastic bag is closed, the can will collapse when air is pumped out of it. The pressure of the air on the outside is strong enough to squeeze the walls together.

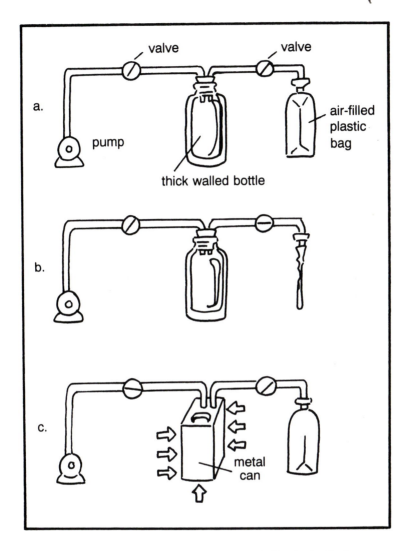

a.

valve   valve

pump

thick walled bottle

air-filled plastic bag

b.

c.

metal can

19a) A sturdy bottle is connected to an air-filled plastic bag on the right and a pump on the left.

b) If air is pumped out of the bottle and the valve between bottle and bag is opened, air will flow from the bag to the bottle.

c) If the bottle is replaced by a can, the can will collapse when air is pumped from it. The arrows show the air pressure pushing the can inward after it has been emptied.

To achieve a similar effect, hold a 1-liter (1-quart) glass bottle with a screw-on cap under a hot water faucet. Fill and empty the bottle several times with hot water. After the final emptying, the air in the bottle should be quite warm. Immediately screw on the cap. Then hold the bottle under cold running water. This won't pump air from the bottle, of course, but it will cause the pressure of the air inside the bottle to decrease. To see that this is true, hold the neck of the bottle next to your ear and slowly open the screw-on cap. You should be able to hear air rushing through the wet opening into the bottle.

4.3   AIR PRESSURE AND COLLAPSING WALLS

To do this experiment you will need:
- adult to help you
- stove
- pail or sink
- clean, empty 1-gallon metal can with screw-on cap or empty soda can
- water
- potholders or oven gloves
- graduated cylinder or measuring cup

You probably don't have a pump like the one shown in Figure 19, but you can do something else to remove air from a can. Find a clean, empty, 1-gallon metal can that has a screw-on cap. Pour about 50 milliliters (2 ounces) of water into the can and leave the top open. **Ask an adult** to help you heat the can on a stove. When the water boils, the steam will displace the air in the can. After the water has been boiling for about 2 minutes, *ask the adult*, who can use a potholder or gloves, to remove the can from the stove and seal it shut by screwing the cap back on the can. Watch the can as it cools. The steam inside will condense to water, but there is no gas to replace the steam. As a result, the pressure inside the can will decrease. What happens to the can as the pressure inside it decreases? Can you explain what you observe?

If you don't have a one-gallon metal can, you can use a soda can. Pour about 10 milliliters (0.5 ounces) of water into the can. *Ask an adult* to heat the can on a stove. After the water has been boiling for about a minute, *ask the adult* to remove the can and quickly turn it upside down in a pail or sink full of cold water. What happens? Can you explain why?

SURPRISE 4.1
Place a balloon inside a narrow-mouth bottle. Pull the mouth of the balloon out over the neck of the bottle, as shown in Figure 20. You will find that you cannot blow up the balloon. Experiment 4.4 will help you explain this surprise.

4.4 AN EXPERIMENT TO INVESTIGATE SURPRISE 4.1

To do this experiment you will need:
- narrow-mouth bottle
- 9- or 12-inch balloon
- plastic drinking straw

Take the bottle and balloon you used in Surprise 4.1 and remove the mouth of the balloon from the neck of the bottle. Leave the round portion of the balloon in the bottle. Now you will find you can blow up the balloon enough to seal the entrance to the bottle.

Next, place a plastic drinking straw in the bottle, as shown in Figure 20b. The top of the straw should project through the bottle's mouth. You will find it quite easy now to blow up the balloon until it fills the bottle.

Having done this experiment, try to explain this surprise. Compare your answer with the one given at the back of the book.

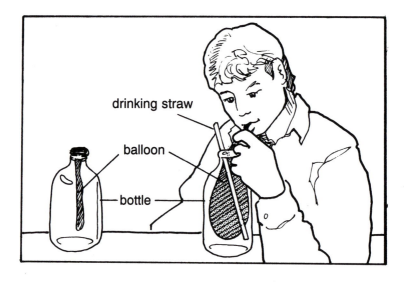

drinking straw

balloon

bottle

20a) Why can't you blow up this balloon?

b) Why does the straw help?

Shifting Air Using Pressure

Find an empty wooden spool such as the kind sewing thread is wound on. These spools have an opening through the center, which is often covered with a round piece of paper. You can also use an empty tube from an old ball point pen or a short piece of small-diameter pipe.

Blow up a balloon until it is quite large. Have a friend hold the neck of the balloon shut or seal it off with a twistie, while you attach it to one end of the spool (see Figure 21). Add only enough air to a second identical balloon to make it firm rather than flaccid. Do not attempt to make it large. Attach it to the other end of the spool.

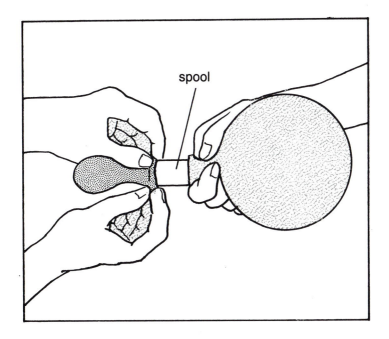

21) What will happen when the balloons are connected through the opening in the spool between them?

4.5 AN EXPERIMENT TO INVESTIGATE SURPRISE 4.2

To do this experiment you will need:
- adult to help you
- 250-milliliter (half-pint) jar
- modeling clay
- food coloring
- balloons (large and small)
- glass tubes and rubber stoppers or plastic drinking straws, and a wooden spool
- large nail
- water
- cooking oil
- twistie
- tape

Building a Pressure Gauge

To compare the pressure of a small balloon with that of a large one, build the pressure "gauge" shown in Figure 22. If you use glass tubes and rubber stoppers, **ask an adult** to help you. A little cooking oil can be used to lubricate the glass so it will slide through the holes in the rubber stoppers easily. A few drops of food coloring will make the water more visible, especially if you use drinking straws that are not made of clear plastic.

You can use modeling clay in place of the two-hole rubber stopper that fits into the mouth of the jar. If you do, use a large nail to make holes in the clay before you insert glass tubes or drinking straws. Then squeeze the clay around the tubes or straws to be sure air can't leak around them. Similarly, a wooden spool can be used in place of the one-hole rubber stopper to connect the balloon to the gauge. Again, clay can be used to seal the spool to the straw. Set the gauge against a wall and tape the top of the tube or straw to the wall.

Before you attach a balloon to the gauge, you will want to be sure that the gauge really does measure gas pressure. You can see that it does by asking a friend to use his or her mouth to apply pressure to the gauge. Your friend should not blow into the tube, but rather apply pressure the way you would if you were trying to start a balloon that is hard to blow up (cheeks should be puffy, not hollow). Water should rise up the long plastic or rubber tube as pressure is applied. The greater the pressure, the higher the liquid will rise.

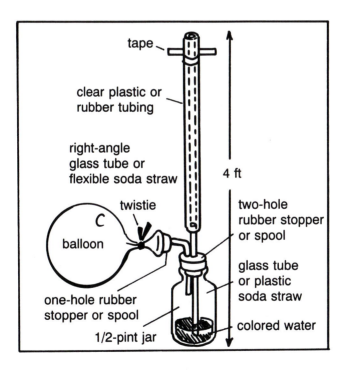

22) This instrument can be used to measure the pressure of gas in a balloon.

Measuring Pressure

After you have seen how the gauge works, attach a small-diameter balloon (one that has been blown up only a little) to the one-hole stopper or spool. Gently release the neck of the balloon so as not to generate any bubbles. The gas pressure in the balloon can now reach the air inside the jar. If the connections are airtight, the balloon will not deflate, but colored water will rise up the long plastic or rubber tube. How high does the water rise when the small balloon is attached? How high does it rise when a large-diameter balloon (one into which a large amount of air has been blown) is attached?

Does this experiment confirm what you found in Surprise 4.2 on page 65? Compare your answer with the first one you gave. How would you explain the surprise now? Compare your answer with the one given at the back of the book.

Will doubling a balloon's thickness increase the pressure it exerts? Will it double the pressure? What do you predict? To test your prediction, put two balloons together as you did in Experiment 2.2c. Use your pressure gauge to compare the pressure of the double-thick balloon with that of a single balloon of the same size. Was your prediction correct?

4.6 PRESSURE AND WATER BALLOONS

To do this experiment you will need:
- 9- or 12-inch balloons
- yardstick
- water
- sink or tub

You have probably made water balloons, so you know

you can put water instead of air in a balloon. To measure the pressure of the water in such a balloon, release the balloon's neck and find the height to which the water rises.

Measuring Water Pressure

Start with a 9- or 12-inch balloon that has been filled with only enough water to make the balloon stretch a little. Hold the balloon in a sink or tub. Ask a friend to hold a yardstick so that its bottom end (the zero mark) is beside the mouth of the balloon, as shown in Figure 23. Carefully release the air at the top of

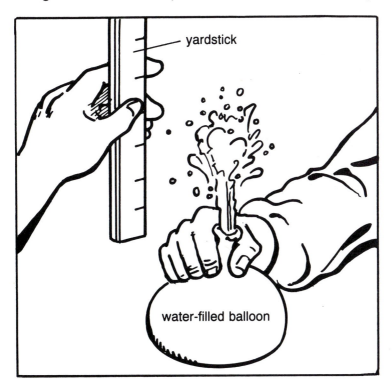

23) Measuring the pressure in a water balloon.

the balloon. Then release the balloon's neck so water can escape. To what height does the water rise?

Repeat the experiment with the same balloon, but this time add enough water to make it very large. From the results of Experiment 4.5, do you expect the water to rise more or less than it did when you released the neck of the small balloon?

Carefully release the air at the top of the balloon. Then, again release the balloon's neck. To what height does the water rise this time? Was your prediction correct?

How do you think the pressure inside one of the smallest balloons you have used (the ones that are so hard to blow up) will compare with those you just tested? How can you test your prediction?

4.7   A BALLOON LUNG

To do this experiment you will need:
- adult to help you
- 9- or 12-inch balloons
- knife
- scissors
- .95-liter (1-quart) plastic soda bottle
- twistie
- plastic drinking straw
- modeling clay
- large rubber band

What Happens When You Breathe

When you breathe in (inhale), the muscles of your diaphragm (which separates your chest from your abdomen) contract and squeeze down on your abdomen, thus increasing the size of your chest. At the same time, your rib cage moves up and outward, which also increases the volume of your chest cavity. When this happens (see Figure 24a), your lungs, which are attached to your chest and diaphragm, get bigger. As your lungs enlarge, the pressure of the air within them decreases. When the pressure in your lungs becomes less than the pressure of the air, air moves through your nose and mouth, through your trachea and bronchial tubes, and into the many air sacs that make up your lungs.

When your diaphragm and chest muscles relax, your chest cavity becomes smaller (see Figure 24b). As the volume of your chest shrinks, the pressure of the air in your lungs becomes greater. When it is greater than air pressure, air moves from your lungs to the air outside your body—you exhale.

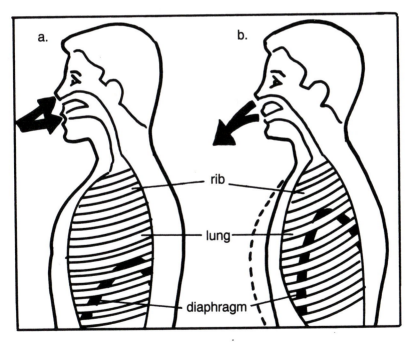

24) The ribs and diaphragm during breathing: (a) inhaling and (b) exhaling.

Making a Model Lung

You can use a balloon to represent a human lung and show how air pressure forces air into your lungs when you breathe. To make a model lung, use a twistie to attach a 9- or 12-inch balloon to a plastic drinking straw (see Figure 25a). The balloon represents a lung. The straw represents the trachea and bronchial tubes leading to the lung. A .95-liter (1-quart) plastic soda bottle can serve as a "chest cavity." **Ask an adult** to cut off the bottom of the bottle. Place the "lung" inside the "chest cavity," and run the "trachea" through the neck of the bottle (see Figure 25b). A piece of modeling clay can be used to close off the mouth of the bottle and hold the straw in place. Finally, use scissors to cut off the

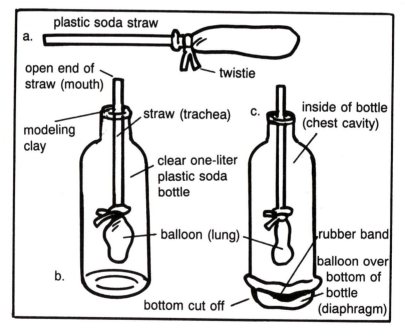

25) These diagrams show you how to make models of (a) a lung, (b) a chest cavity, and (c) a diaphragm.

neck of a 12-inch balloon and pull it over the bottom of the bottle. This balloon, over the bottom of the bottle, represents your diaphragm, which moves up and down when you breathe. A large rubber band can be used to hold the "diaphragm" in place (see Figure 25c).

What happens to the lung when you pull the "diaphragm" down? When you release the diaphragm or push it a short way into the "chest cavity" (bottle)? What happens to the pressure inside the bottle when you increase the bottle's volume by pulling down on the diaphragm? Where does the air come from that inflates the balloon? What happens to the pressure in the bottle and around the "lung" when you push the diaphragm into the bottle?

This model is different than a real chest cavity. It has a diaphragm, but it has no rib cage. See if you can design and build a model that takes into account the movement of the ribs as well as the diaphragm.

4.8 PRESSURE AND A BALLOON ROCKET

To do this experiment you will need:

- plastic drinking straw
- tape
- new pencil with eraser
- 2-liter (half-gallon) cardboard milk carton
- thread
- twisties
- bicycle tire pump
- round and oblong balloons
- tub

Building an Air-Powered Rocket

You can use a balloon to make an air-powered rocket. Mount a plastic drinking straw on a long thread, as shown in Figure 26a. Blow up an oblong balloon, seal its neck with a twistie, and attach it to the straw with tape, as shown in Figure 26b. Hold the neck of the balloon shut as you remove the twistie. What happens when you release the balloon?

How does size affect your balloon rocket? To find

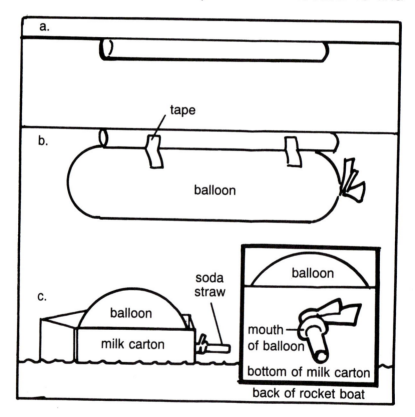

26a) Mount a plastic drinking straw on a long thread.

b) Attach an oblong balloon to the straw with tape.

c) This rocket boat exhausts its fuel through the straw.

out, use a bicycle tire pump to put different amounts of air in the balloon. Will a rocket with twice as much "fuel" travel twice as far? Will it travel twice as fast?

Build a double-layered balloon rocket (see Experiment 2.2c). What effect does a thicker wall have on your balloon rocket? Does it travel twice as far? Does it travel twice as fast? Will a round balloon travel as fast or as far as an oblong balloon if both contain the same amount of air? Does the shape of the balloon have any effect on your rocket? Can you explain why? Hint: remember Science Principle: Air Resistance and Area in Chapter 3.

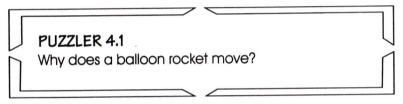

PUZZLER 4.1
Why does a balloon rocket move?

Building a Rocket-Powered Boat

Use an empty half-gallon cardboard milk carton, tape, and a balloon to build a rocket-powered boat (see Figure 26c). Will the boat move faster, farther, or for a longer time if the air exhausts through a drinking straw rather than through the open neck of the balloon? Will its motion be improved in any way if the end of the straw is under water?

During the 1930s, lighter-than-air ships (Zeppelins) carried passengers across the Atlantic Ocean. These Zeppelins consisted of a rigid, fabric-covered frame that was filled with hydrogen to make it buoyant. Some people were afraid to travel in such ships because hydrogen will burn. If ignited, hydrogen combines with the oxygen in air to form water vapor. Their fears were well-founded. On the evening of May 6, 1937, thirty-six people died when the Hindenburg, the largest and most luxurious of these German Zeppelins, caught fire while mooring at Lakehurst, New Jersey. Since that time, helium not hydrogen (which is lighter but flammable) has been used in lighter-than-air ships.

Balloons: A Science in Themselves

In earlier chapters you used balloons to learn about density; to compare the properties of various gases, with an emphasis on helium; and to investigate the effect of temperature and pressure on gases. In this chapter, you will use balloons in a number of other experiments involving sound, Bernoulli's principle, electric charge, freezing, and motion.

Science Principle: Sound Comes from Vibrations

Sound arises when a vibrating object pushes air back and forth. You can see this for yourself by "plucking" a rigid plastic or wooden ruler. Place the ruler on a table so that about half of it extends beyond the edge. Use one hand to hold the ruler firmly against the top of the table. Use the other hand to pluck the end of the ruler that extends beyond the edge. You will see the ruler vibrate and produce a sound. What happens to the pitch of the sound as you increase the length of the ruler that vibrates beyond the edge of the table? What happens to the pitch of the sound as you reduce the length of the ruler that vibrates?

PUZZLER 5.1
What causes the vibrations that allow you to make noises when you speak?

5.1 BALLOONS AS SOUND MAKERS

To do this experiment you will need:
- 9- or 12-inch balloons
- musical instrument (if possible)

Blow up a balloon. Ask a friend to talk to you as you hold the balloon in front of his or her mouth. You will feel the air in the balloon vibrating as your friend talks. Can you explain why you feel these vibrations?

What happens to the vibrations when your friend speaks loudly? When he or she sings or plays a musical instrument near the balloon you are holding?

Blow up a balloon. Hold the neck of the balloon by grasping its opposite sides with the thumbs and index fingers of your two hands. Watch the mouth of the balloon closely as you release the air rather quickly. Can you see what is vibrating to cause the sound you hear?

Repeat the experiment, but this time stretch the neck so the air is released slowly (see Figure 27). Is the sound you hear different than before? Can you find what is vibrating to produce the sound you hear this time?

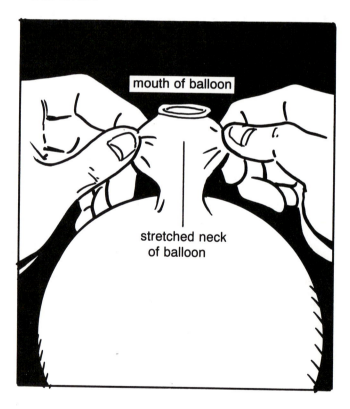

27) Make balloon sounds!

Science Principle: Bernoulli's Principle

Suppose a fluid, be it a liquid or gas, is flowing through a tube, as shown in Figure 28. If the same amount of fluid enters and leaves the tube each second, then the fluid must flow faster through the narrow, middle part of the tube. If it didn't, the fluid would back up. The pressure gauges show that the pressure is least where the fluid flows fastest. The pressure is greatest where the fluid flows slowest. This relationship between the pressure of a fluid and its speed of flow is known as Bernoulli's principle.

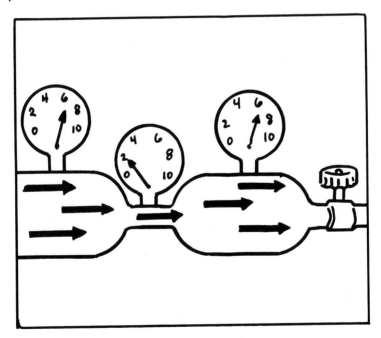

28) When a fluid flows fast, its pressure is less than when it flows more slowly.

5.2   BALLOONS AND BERNOULLI

To do this experiment you will need:
- 9- or 12-inch balloons
- string or thread

Blow up two 9- or 12-inch balloons. Suspend them from strings or threads so that they hang side by side about a foot apart (see Figure 29a). Blow lung air between the two balloons. What happens? How

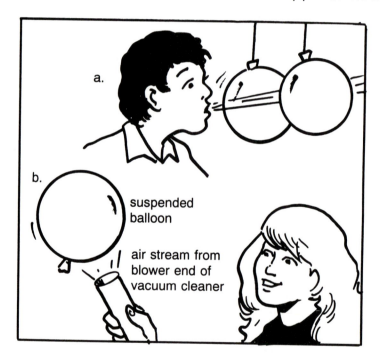

a.

b.

suspended balloon

air stream from blower end of vacuum cleaner

29a) What happens when you blow air between two balloons suspended from threads?

b) A balloon can be suspended in a stream of air.

can you use Bernoulli's principle to explain what you observe?

What do you think will happen if you blow a stream of air to the left of the balloon on your left? If you blow a stream of air to the right of the balloon on your right? Test your predictions. Were you right?

PUZZLER 5.2
Blow air into a balloon until it is about 12 centimeters (5 inches) in diameter. Tie off the neck of the balloon to seal the air inside. Arrange the blower end of a vacuum cleaner or hair dryer to produce an air stream that is directed straight upward. (If you use a hair dryer, turn off the heater coils.) If you place the balloon in the air stream, it will stay there. If you slowly turn the stream so it shoots sideways, as well as upward (Figure 29b), the balloon defies gravity and remains in the stream. How can you explain the balloon's puzzling behavior? Compare your explanation with the one on page 97.

Science Principle: Electric Charge

Benjamin Franklin rubbed a rubber rod with cat's fur and suspended it in a sling, like the one shown in Figure 30a. He found that if he stroked a second rubber rod with fur and held it near the rod in the sling, the

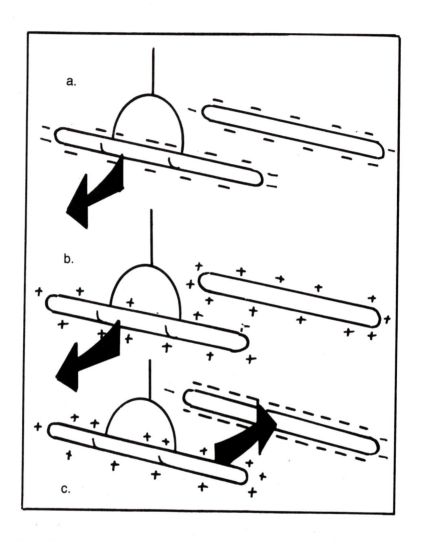

30a) Two rubber rods that have been rubbed with fur repel one another. Both have a negative (–) charge.

b) Two glass rods rubbed with silk repel one another. Both have a positive (+) charge.

c) A glass rod (+) and a rubber rod (–) attract one another.

two rods would repel one another. He reasoned that since both rods had been charged in the same way, they must carry the same charge. He defined the charge on the rubber rod to be negative.

When Franklin rubbed a glass rod with silk and suspended it in a sling (see Figure 30b), he found, as expected, that it was repelled by another glass rod that had been rubbed with silk. But when he held the glass rod near the suspended rubber rod, the two rods attracted one another (see Figure 30c). He argued that the glass rod had a different charge than the rubber rod. He defined the charge on the glass rod to be positive.

Glass rods charged in the same way repel one another. Rubber rods charged in the same way repel one another. But a charged rubber rod is attracted by a charged glass rod. Franklin concluded that like charges (+ and + or – and –) repel one another, and unlike charges (+ and –) attract one another.

Other objects were rubbed with various materials and held near charged rubber or glass rods. It was found that objects that attracted the rubber rod repelled the glass rod. Objects that attracted the glass rod repelled the rubber rod. This indicated that there were only two kinds of charges—positive (+) and negative (–).

5.3 BALLOONS AND ELECTRIC CHARGE

To do this experiment you will need:
- 9- or 12-inch balloons
- marking pen
- clear plastic tape
- string or thread
- cloth
- water faucet

Separating Charges

(This experiment should be done on a cool, clear, dry day. Electric charges leak away quickly in warm, damp air.) Blow up a balloon. Suspend it from a string or thread. Dry your hands thoroughly before you use a marking pen to draw a circle on one side of the balloon. Then rub the circled area of the balloon with a piece of cloth. If you have successfully separated charges, the balloon should have one charge and the cloth the opposite charge. To see if this has happened, move the cloth slowly toward the circled side of the balloon. Is the balloon attracted or repelled by the cloth? Do the charges on the balloon and cloth have the same or opposite signs?

Inflate a second balloon to match the first. Draw a circle on one side of this balloon and charge it in the same way as before. Bring the two charged circular areas near each other. What happens when you bring the circled area on the first balloon near the circled area on the second balloon?

Watch the string or thread connected to the

suspended balloon as you bring the second charged balloon closer. The angle of the string will help you observe how much the balloon is pushed. Does the distance between the balloons have any effect on the size of the push one charged balloon exerts on the other?

Opposite Charges

The same material can sometimes carry opposite charges. To see that this is true, cut off a piece of clear plastic tape about 20 centimeters (8 inches) long. Attach one end to the top of a chair or cabinet. Cut off a second piece of tape and bring it near the first piece. Do the two pieces of tape carry like or unlike charges? How do you know?

Fold over one end on each of the two strips. The folded ends provide little handles that will allow you to pick up the strips without having them stick to you. Hang one of the strips, as you did before, with the nonsticky side facing you. Place the sticky side of the second strip on the nonsticky side of the first strip—the strip that is hanging. Use the little handles you made to pull the two strips apart.

Determining Same and Opposite Charges

Again, hang one of the strips from a chair or cabinet. Hold the second strip so it is parallel to the one you suspended and slowly bring it close to the suspended strip. Are the charges on the strip the same or opposite? How can you tell?

Bring one of the two strips of oppositely charged tape near the circled area of the hanging balloon. Does the circled area turn toward or away from the strip? Is the charge on the tape the same or opposite in sign to that on the balloon? What do you predict will happen if you bring the other strip of tape near the circle on the balloon? Will the circle turn toward or away from the strip? Try it! Were you right? Is the charge on this strip of tape the same or opposite in sign to that on the circled part of the balloon?

Blow up a balloon and rub it with the same cloth you used to charge the suspended balloon. Bring the charged balloon close to (but don't touch) a thin stream of water flowing from a faucet. Does water respond to a charged object? Since water is not charged, how can you explain the attraction between water and the charged balloon?

5.4 BALLOONS AND INDUCED CHARGE

To do this experiment you will need:
- 9- or 12-inch balloons
- cloth
- pie tin
- string or thread
- glass or plastic bottle

Blow up a balloon, charge it by rubbing it with a cloth, and hang it from a thread or string. Bring your hand near the balloon. As you can see, the balloon is attracted to your hand. Perhaps this is because some of the charge on the cloth remains on your hand. Ask a friend who has not touched the cloth to hold his or her hand near the balloon. Is the balloon attracted to your friend's hand?

Hold a glass or plastic bottle near the balloon. Is the balloon attracted to the glass or bottle? Will a metal pie tin attract the balloon?

SURPRISE 5.1
What do you think will happen if you hold the plastic strip that repels the balloon near a thin stream of water, as shown in Figure 31. Watch closely as the tape gets close to the water. You should see the stream bend toward the tape. If you have difficulty seeing the effect, repeat the experiment with a freshly charged strip.

What do you think will happen if you hold the plastic strip that attracts the balloon near a thin stream of water?

What surprises you? How can you explain the fact that both pieces of plastic attract the water even though their charges are opposite? Compare your explanation with the one found on page 97.

Equal Charges

A charged object, such as a balloon that has been rubbed with a cloth, is attracted to other objects that have not been charged. Even if an object has not been charged by rubbing, like all matter it has an electric charge. It simply has equal amounts of positive and negative charges. Usually, the uncharged object has some charges that can move. Suppose you bring an object that has no excess of either positive or negative charges near a negatively charged balloon, like the one shown in Figure 32. The negative

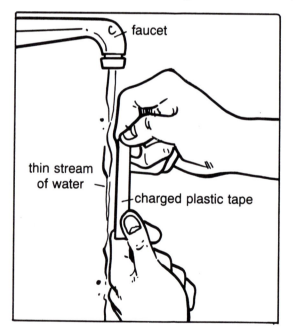

faucet

thin stream of water

charged plastic tape

31) What happens when a piece of charged plastic tape is held parallel to a thin stream of water?

charges in the object will move as far from the balloon as possible. At the same time, the positive charges in the balloon will move as close to the balloon as possible. As you have seen, electric forces increase when charges are closer together. Since the unlike charges (negative and positive) are closer than the like charges, attraction will be stronger than repulsion.

Charge a balloon by rubbing it with a cloth. Then

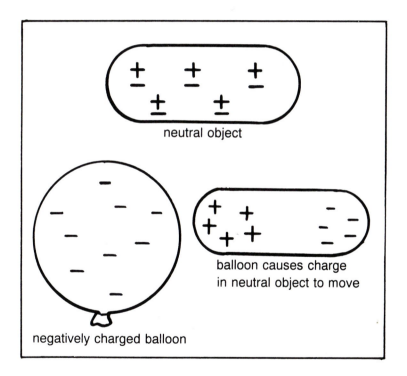

neutral object

balloon causes charge
in neutral object to move

negatively charged balloon

32) A charged balloon will cause charges to move in an uncharged object.

hold the balloon against a wall. The balloon will stick to the wall. How can you explain this?

In Experiment 2.2b you were able to control a helium-filled balloon's motion with your hand. How was that possible?

5.5   A FROZEN BALLOON

To do this experiment you will need:
- 9- or 12-inch balloons
- water
- tape measure
- freezer

Fill a 9- or 12-inch balloon with water until it is about the size of an orange. Tie off the balloon and have a friend hold the water balloon in his or her hand while you measure its circumference (the distance around the balloon's "equator") with a tape measure. Record the balloon's circumference. Then place the water balloon in a freezer overnight.

On the following day, when the water is thoroughly frozen, measure the balloon's circumference again. What has happened to the volume inside the balloon? What happens to water when it freezes?

PUZZLER 5.3
Based on what you learned in the previous experiment and what you learned in Chapter 1, why does ice float in water?

5.6   A BALLOON CAR AND FRICTIONLESS MOTION

To do this experiment you will need:

- adult to help you
- hammer
- glue
- 9- or 12-inch balloons
- cloth
- smooth surface such as the top of a kitchen counter
- small sharp nail
- small blocks of wood
- wooden spool
- toothpick
- smooth board
- plastic drinking straw
- metal jar lid—8 centimeters (3 inches) across

Newton's First Law of Motion

In the 1600s, Sir Isaac Newton explained motion in terms that apply to the entire universe. His First Law of Motion states that an object in motion will continue to move at a steady speed forever unless a force acts on it. On earth, a common force that acts on moving objects is *friction*. If you give a toy car or wagon a push, it moves in the direction you push it. But it soon slows and comes to a stop as friction between the wheels and the floor push against the motion.

Building a Balloon Car

To see how something moves when there is very little friction—the kind of motion that Newton visualized— you can build a balloon car that floats on a cushion of air. Find a smooth, metal jar lid about 8 centimeters

(3 inches) across. **Ask an adult** to help you punch a small hole through the exact center of the top of the jar lid by using a small, sharp nail and a hammer. To avoid bending the metal, place the lid on a small block of wood, as shown in Figure 33.

Glue a wooden spool to the bottom of the metal lid. Be sure the hole in the lid lines up with the hole in the spool. When the glue has dried, place the lid and spool on a smooth surface such as the top of a kitchen counter. Attach an inflated balloon to the spool. Air flowing from the balloon through the spool and out the hole in the jar lid should form a cushion of air under the lid. Since the balloon car floats on a cushion of air, there should be very little friction between it and the counter top.

Give the car a gentle push. Notice how smoothly it moves without any sign of slowing down. (If it does not move at nearly constant speed, you may have to make the nail hole slightly larger.) Which way must you push on the car to stop it?

A hot-air balloon floats in air. The direction it moves depends on the wind. You can see a similar effect by using a plastic drinking straw to blow on a balloon car. What happens when a "wind" pushes your balloon car? What happens when you change the wind direction?

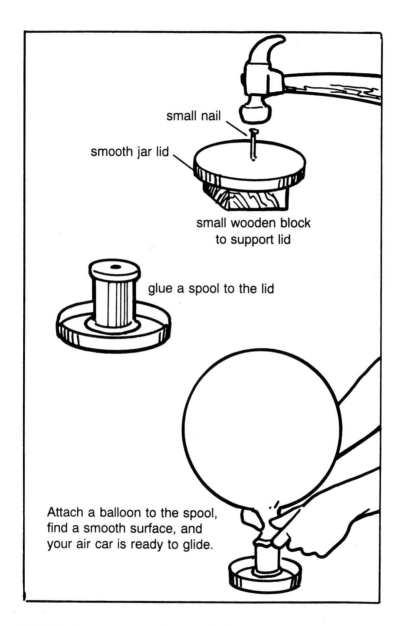

small nail

smooth jar lid

small wooden block
to support lid

glue a spool to the lid

Attach a balloon to the spool,
find a smooth surface, and
your air car is ready to glide.

33) A balloon car can be made from a jar lid, a spool,
and a balloon.

Inflicting a Force on an Object

You have seen that if nothing pushes or pulls on an object, it moves at a steady speed along a straight line. To see what happens when something continues to push on an object, use the drinking straw to blow steadily on the balloon car as it moves along a straight line. What happens to the speed of the car as you keep blowing on it in a fixed direction?

Place a block under one end of a smooth board that is resting on a level counter or floor. Put the balloon car on the board and release it. Which way does the car move? What happens to the car's speed as it moves?

Repeat the experiment with a toothpick, not a block, under one end of board. How can you tell which end of the board is supported by the toothpick? How can you use the balloon car to tell whether or not a surface is level?

PUZZLER 5.4

What force is acting on the balloon car to make its speed increase as it moves down the slanted board? If possible, build two balloon cars. Charge each balloon by rubbing them with a cloth. What do you think will happen if you push one charged balloon car toward the other? Try it! Were you right?

Answers to Puzzlers and Surprises

Puzzler 1.1

If the clay is molded into the shape of a boat or a hollow ball, it will float. Together, the clay and the air within the sides of the boat weigh less than an equal volume of water. The clay and the air together are less dense than water. The same is true of a concrete or a steel ship.

Puzzler 3.1

In addition to extinguishing flames, carbon dioxide tends to come down around a fire because it is more dense than air. It surrounds the fire and prevents air from reaching the flames. Since helium is much less dense than air, it would rise above the fire.

Surprise 3.1

The balls side by side and strike the floor at very nearly the same instant.

Surprise 4.1

There is air in the bottle. When you try to blow up the balloon, the pressure of the air inside the bottle increases because you are trying to squeeze it into a smaller space. This increased pressure pushes back against the outside walls of the balloon as you try to increase the pressure against the inside of the same walls. Putting a straw in the bottle, next to the balloon, allows the air in the bottle to escape. As the volume of the balloon increases, air in the bottle leaves through the straw.

Surprise 4.2

The pressure of the air inside a balloon that has been blown up to a large diameter is smaller than the pressure inside the same balloon when it is only slightly blown up. Just think how much harder you have to blow to get a balloon started than you do when it is quite large.

Puzzler 4.1

When you release the balloon, the gas pressure at the open neck of the balloon is the pressure of the air around the balloon. The pressure on the front of the balloon is the pressure of the air inside the balloon. Since the pressure inside the balloon is greater than the pressure of the air outside the balloon, there is a greater force pushing the balloon forward than backward.

Puzzler 5.1

The vocal cords in your voice box (Adam's apple) vibrate when air passes over them. Notice that when you speak or sing, you exhale air from your lungs.

Puzzler 5.2

The explanation lies in Bernoulli's principle. Should the balloon stray to the edge of the air stream where the velocity of the air is less, the pressure there will be greater than in the middle of the stream where the air moves faster. Since higher pressure is found at the outer edges of the air stream, the balloon always gets pushed back toward the center of the stream when it strays sideways. The inward push on the balloon due to pressure differences is enough to balance at least part of the balloon's weight.

Surprise 5.1

Charges within the water are induced to move. When a negatively charged object is held near the water stream, the positive charges in the water move toward it; the negative charges move away. When a positive charge is held near the stream, the reverse is true. The charges in the water and the charged object that are closest will always be opposite in sign. Since electrical forces decrease with distance, the attractive force between water and the charged object will always be greater than the repelling force.

Puzzler 5.3

When water freezes, its volume increases. This tells you that ice takes up more space than the same weight of water. Therefore, ice is less dense than water. Because water is less dense as a solid (ice) than as a liquid, ice floats in water.

Puzzler 5.4

The force of gravity pulls the car down the board just as it would pull an automobile or a bicycle down a hill. Since the two balloons have the same charge, they will repel one another.

Further Reading

Adler, Irene. *Ballooning: High and Wild*. Mahwah, N.J.: Troll, 1976.

Chandra, Deborah. *Balloons*. New York: Farrar, Strauss & Giroux, 1990.

Costanzo, Christie. *Hot Air Ballooning*. Mankato, Minn.: Capstone Press, 1991.

Grummer, Arnold E. *The Great Balloon Game Book and More Balloon Activities*. Appleton, Wis.: Markim, Greg, Publishers, 1987.

Kaner, Etta. *Balloon Science*. Reading, Mass.: Addison Wesley, 1990.

Richards, Norman. *Giants in the Sky*. Chicago: Childrens Press, 1967.

Scarry, Huck. *Balloon Trip, A Sketchbook*. Englewood Cliffs, N.J.: Prentice-Hall, 1982.

Wirth, Dick. *Ballooning: A Complete Guide to Riding the Winds*. New York: McKay, 1991.

Zubrowski, Bernie. *Balloons: Building and Experimenting with Inflatable Toys*. New York: Morrow, 1990.

Index

About the Authors

Robert Gardner is a retired high school teacher of physics, chemistry, and physical science. He has taught in a number of National Science Foundation teachers' institutes and is an award-winning author of science books for young people.

David Webster was a former elementary and middle school science teacher. For several years he wrote a regular feature for *Nature and Science* magazine.